ALL ABOUT ME

WRITTEN BY.........ME
directed by ....ME
PRODUCED BY..........ME

Once upon a time, in real life there was a baby born and that baby was **ME...**

I WAS BORN ON _____

IN THIS PLACE _____

I HAVE _____ **BROTHERS +** _____ **SISTERS.**

my hair is _____ *and my eyes are* _____

☆ IMPORTANT INFORMATION! ☆

⇩ ⇩ ⇩

HELLO
MY NAME IS

6 FT —

5 FT —

4 FT —

3 FT —

I'M THIS TALL

MY FAVORITE COLOR

MY SECOND FAVORITE COLOR

MY AGE:_____

i live in:

TODAY'S DATE

MY FAVORITES

BOOK _____

MOVIE _____

DAY OF THE WEEK _____

MONTH _____

SEASON _____

SONG _____

MUSICIAN _____

SPORT _____

SUBJECT IN SCHOOL _____

RESTAURANT _____

PLACE IN THE WORLD _____

PLACE IN MY HOME _____

SWEET TREAT _____

SALTY TREAT _____

HOLIDAY _____

SCENT _____

STORE _____

THING TO WEAR _____

SUMMER ACTIVITY _____

WINTER ACTIVITY _____

ME

☆ My Accomplishments ☆

Today:

This week:

This month:

This year:

In My Life:

3 Things that Im really good at:

3 really good qualities I have:

I deserve a Trophy!

(Write your name and your award and color it)

My family and friends deserve trophies too!

(Write their names and what their trophy is for!)

Today's Date: _____

MY RANDOM THOUGHTS

_____

_____

_____

_____

_____

_____

_____

_____

_____

_____

_____

_____

_____

_____

_____

_____

_____

ME + ANIMALS

Animals I think are cute:

Animals I think are amazing:

Animals I would like as a pet:

Animals I would not like as a pet:

If I were an animal I would be a:
         because...

If I had a pet elephant I would name him:
If I had a pet seal I would name her:
If I had a pet monkey I would name him:
If I had a pet frog I would name her:
If I had a pet parrot I would name her:
If I had a pet kangaroo I would name him:
If I had a pet goat I would name him:

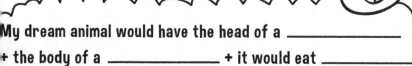

My dream animal would have the head of a _____
+ the body of a _____ + it would eat _____
+ be really good at _____

CURIOUS ME

Things I wonder about...and questions I have...

MY FAMILY
TREE

ADD YOUR FAMILY MEMBERS. YOU CAN ADD MORE FRAMES IF YOU WANT.
AUNTS, UNCLES, COUSINS, FRIENDS, AND DOGS ARE FAMILY TOO!

MY GOALS

Today:

This week:

This month:

This year:

In My Life:

3 Things that I want to learn:

A job that I think I would be great at:

MY HAIR

WHEN I WAKE UP

AFTER IT GETS BRUSHED

WHEN ITS FANCY

IN MY DREAMS

ME + TRAVELING

I HAVE TRAVELED BY

   MY FAVORITE WAY TO
TRAVEL IS BY: _____

 PLACES I HAVE BEEN TO:

FUN THINGS I HAVE DONE WHILE TRAVELING:

GREAT FOOD I ATE:

WHAT I LIKE ABOUT TRAVELING:

 PLACES I WANT TO VISIT:

SOMETHING NEW I WANT TO TRY WHILE TRAVELING:

MY FOOD ADVENTURES

There are some foods I love, like _____ , _____ , _____ , and _____ . Then there are some foods I really don't like! For example: _____ and _____ . But there are also some foods that I never tried, like _____ and _____ . The weirdest food I ever tried was _____ and I thought it was _____ !

To me, this food smells delicious: _____
and this food smells gross! : _____
A food I really want to try is: _____

If I had to eat the same thing for breakfast every day I would eat:

_____

If I had to eat the same thing for lunch every day I would eat:

_____

If I had to eat the same thing for dinner every night I would eat:

_____

If I could travel to any country and taste all the food I would choose:

_____

If I was writing a children's book about 1 type of food, it would be about:

_____

and the title of the book would be:

_____

If I was a fruit or a vegetable I would be: _____ because...

♪ ♫ ME + MUSIC ♬

MY PLAYLIST:
1.
2.
3.
4.
5.
6.
7.
8.

FAVORITE ARTISTS:
1.
2.
3.
4.
5.
6.
7.
8.

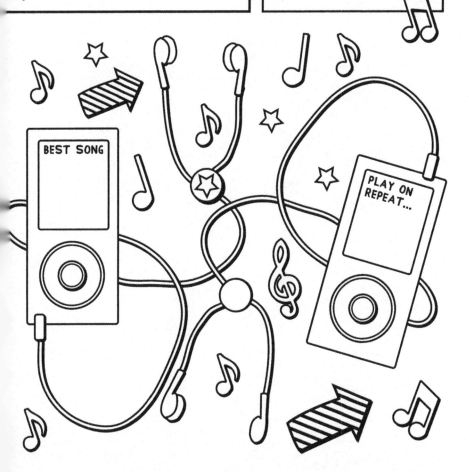

BEST SONG

PLAY ON REPEAT...

Today's Date : _____

MY HAPPY THOUGHTS

MY HOBBIES

☀ **OUTDOOR DAYTIME HOBBIES**

☂ **INDOOR RAINY DAY HOBBIES**

☾ **NIGHT TIME HOBBIES**

😎 **EVERYTHING ELSE**

MY MOVIE

TITLE......................................
WRITTEN BY................................
DIRECTED BY...............................
PRODUCED BY...............................

TYPE OF MOVIE

- ☐ ANIMATED
- ☐ COMEDY
- ☐ MYSTERY
- ☐ ACTION
- ☐ DRAMA
- ☐ ROMANCE
- ☐ HORROR
- ☐

WHEN DOES IT TAKE PLACE?

- ☐ PRESENT DAY
- ☐ FUTURE
- ☐ 1970'S-80'S
- ☐ 1950'S-60'S
- ☐ 200 YRS AGO
- ☐ 1000 YRS AGO
- ☐

WHO IS IN IT

- ☐ HUMANS
- ☐ ANIMALS
- ☐ MONSTERS
- ☐ VAMPIRES
- ☐ MAGICAL CREATURES
- ☐

STARRING:

....AS
....AS
....AS
....AS
....AS
....AS
....AS
....AS

SETTING: (WHERE AND WHEN)

MY MOVIE
(CONTINUED)

WHAT IS IT ABOUT?

MAIN CHARACTER:

CONFLICT:

RESOLUTION:

LESSON OR MORAL:

POP CORN

Today's Date : _____

MY RANDOM THOUGHTS

_____

_____

_____

_____

_____

_____

_____

_____

_____

_____

_____

_____

_____

_____

_____

_____

MY TELEVISION SERIES

Show Name:

Starring ME as : ☆   ☆

Other characters:

Type of Tv Show:

Takes place here:

In this year:

The show is about:

It's entertaining because:

I love it because:

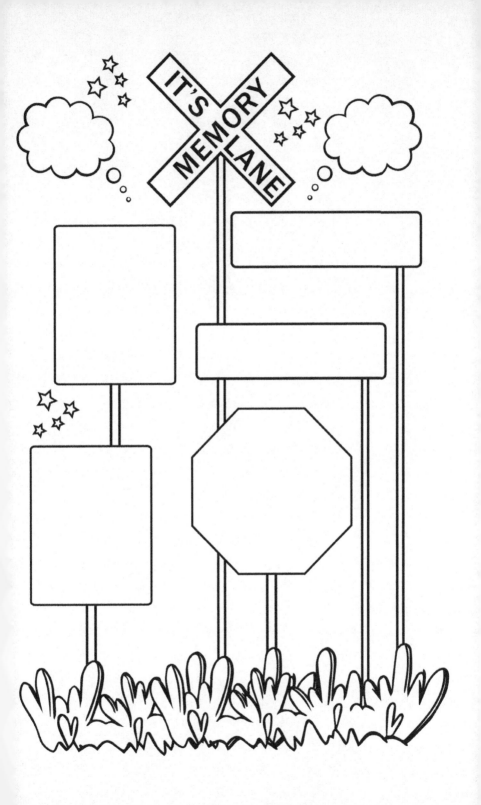

SCHOOL STUFF

SCHOOL NAME:

MY GRADE:

FAVORITE SUBJECTS:

I'M GREAT AT:

I LIKE SCHOOL BECAUSE...

MY FRIENDS

write about your friends. draw their faces and hair too!
Friends can also be members of your family

NAME:
AGE:
WHERE WE MET:
FUN FACTS:

NAME:
AGE:
WHERE WE MET:
FUN FACTS:

NAME:
AGE:
WHERE WE MET:
FUN FACTS:

NAME:
AGE:
WHERE WE MET:
FUN FACTS:

NAME:
AGE:
WHERE WE MET:
FUN FACTS:

NAME:
AGE:
WHERE WE MET:
FUN FACTS:

Today's Date : _____

MY HAPPY THOUGHTS

_____

_____

_____

_____

_____

_____

_____

_____

_____

_____

_____

_____

_____

_____

MY HAPPY THOUGHT!

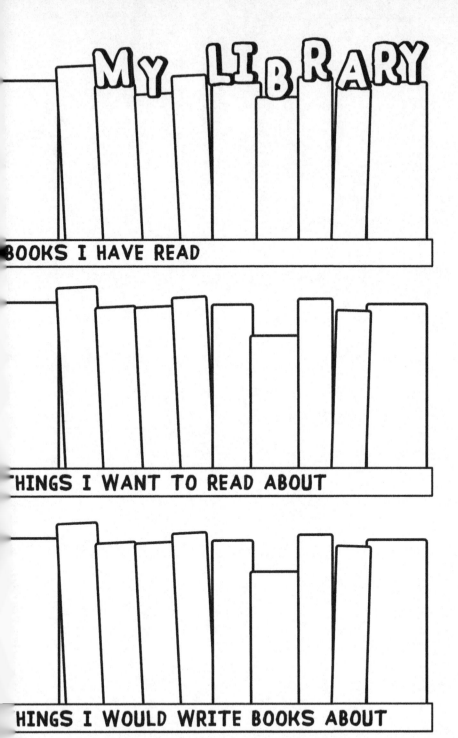

MY LIBRARY

BOOKS I HAVE READ

THINGS I WANT TO READ ABOUT

THINGS I WOULD WRITE BOOKS ABOUT

(TURN THIS BOOK SIDEWAYS TO WRITE ON THE BOOKS)

I would like to get first prize ribbons for these 4 things

MY DREAM DAY

On my dream day the weather would be...

Today's Date : _____

MY RANDOM THOUGHTS

_____

_____

_____

_____

_____

_____

_____

_____

_____

_____

_____

_____

_____

_____

_____

_____

MY RANDOM THOUGHTS

ME + BLUE

The color Blue makes me feel:

MY FAVORITE BLUE THING IS:

On a scale of 1 to 10 I like Blue:

1 2 3 4 5 6 7 8 9 10

(lowest)   (highest)

I would choose Blue for:

- ☐ Car
- ☐ House
- ☐ Bedroom
- ☐ Sneakers
- ☐ Shirt
- ☐ Jacket
- ☐ Backpack
- ☐ Phone Cover
- ☐ Flowers

Blue makes me think of...

ME + RED

The color red makes me feel:

MY FAVORITE RED THING IS:

On a scale of 1 to 10 I like red:

1 2 3 4 5 6 7 8 9 10

(lowest)   (highest)

I would choose red for:

- ☐ Car
- ☐ House
- ☐ Bedroom
- ☐ Sneakers
- ☐ Shirt
- ☐ Jacket
- ☐ Backpack
- ☐ Phone Cover
- ☐ Flowers

red makes me think of...

ME + GREEN

The color green makes me feel:

MY FAVORITE GREEN THING IS:

On a scale of 1 to 10 I like Green:

1 2 3 4 5 6 7 8 9 10

(lowest)   (highest)

would choose green for:

- ☐ Car
- ☐ House
- ☐ Bedroom
- ☐ Sneakers
- ☐ Shirt
- ☐ Jacket
- ☐ Backpack
- ☐ Phone Cover
- ☐ Flowers

green makes me think of. . .

ME + YELLOW

The color yellow makes me feel:

MY FAVORITE YELLOW THING IS:

On a scale of 1 to 10 I like Yellow:

1   2   3   4   5   6   7   8   9   10

(lowest)   (highest)

I would choose yellow for:

- ☐ Car
- ☐ House
- ☐ Bedroom
- ☐ Sneakers
- ☐ Shirt
- ☐ Jacket
- ☐ Backpack
- ☐ Phone Cover
- ☐ Flowers

yellow makes me think of...

ME + PINK

The color pink makes me feel:

MY FAVORITE PINK THING IS:

On a scale of 1 to 10 I like Pink:

1 2 3 4 5 6 7 8 9 10
(lowest)   (highest)

I would choose pink for:
- ☐ Car
- ☐ House
- ☐ Bedroom
- ☐ Sneakers
- ☐ Shirt
- ☐ Jacket
- ☐ Backpack
- ☐ Phone Cover
- ☐ Flowers

pink makes me think of. . .

ME + BROWN

The color brown makes me feel:

MY FAVORITE BROWN THING IS:

On a scale of 1 to 10 I like Brown:

1 2 3 4 5 6 7 8 9 10
(lowest)   (highest)

I would choose Brown for:

- ☐ Car
- ☐ House
- ☐ Bedroom
- ☐ Sneakers
- ☐ Shirt
- ☐ Jacket
- ☐ Backpack
- ☐ Phone Cover
- ☐ Flowers

Brown makes me think of...

ME + BLACK

The color black makes me feel:

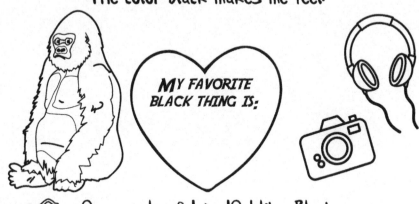

MY FAVORITE BLACK THING IS:

On a scale of 1 to 10 I like Black:

1 2 3 4 5 6 7 8 9 10
(lowest)   (highest)

I would choose black for:

- ☐ Car
- ☐ House
- ☐ Bedroom
- ☐ Sneakers
- ☐ Shirt
- ☐ Jacket
- ☐ Backpack
- ☐ Phone Cover
- ☐ Flowers

black makes me think of...

ME + WHITE

The color White makes me feel:

MY FAVORITE WHITE THING IS:

On a scale of 1 to 10 I like White:

1 2 3 4 5 6 7 8 9 10

(lowest)   (highest)

I would choose White for:

- ☐ Car
- ☐ House
- ☐ Bedroom
- ☐ Sneakers
- ☐ Shirt
- ☐ Jacket
- ☐ Backpack
- ☐ Phone Cover
- ☐ Flowers

White makes me think of...

MY MOVIE REVIEWS

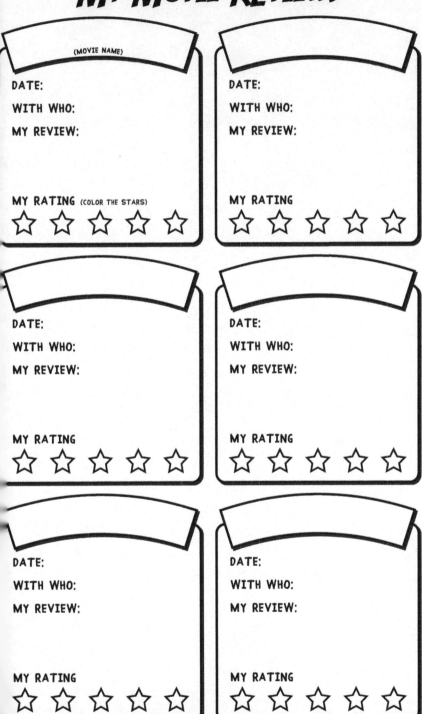

(MOVIE NAME)

DATE:

WITH WHO:

MY REVIEW:

MY RATING (COLOR THE STARS)
☆ ☆ ☆ ☆ ☆

DATE:

WITH WHO:

MY REVIEW:

MY RATING
☆ ☆ ☆ ☆ ☆

DATE:

WITH WHO:

MY REVIEW:

MY RATING
☆ ☆ ☆ ☆ ☆

DATE:

WITH WHO:

MY REVIEW:

MY RATING
☆ ☆ ☆ ☆ ☆

DATE:

WITH WHO:

MY REVIEW:

MY RATING
☆ ☆ ☆ ☆ ☆

DATE:

WITH WHO:

MY REVIEW:

MY RATING
☆ ☆ ☆ ☆ ☆

MY BOOK REVIEWS

(BOOK NAME)

WHEN I READ IT:

MY REVIEW:

MY RATING (COLOR THE STARS)
☆ ☆ ☆ ☆ ☆

WHEN I READ IT:

MY REVIEW:

MY RATING
☆ ☆ ☆ ☆ ☆

WHEN I READ IT:

MY REVIEW:

MY RATING
☆ ☆ ☆ ☆ ☆

WHEN I READ IT:

MY REVIEW:

MY RATING
☆ ☆ ☆ ☆ ☆

WHEN I READ IT:

MY REVIEW:

MY RATING
☆ ☆ ☆ ☆ ☆

WHEN I READ IT:

MY REVIEW:

MY RATING
☆ ☆ ☆ ☆ ☆

MY RESTAURANT REVIEWS

(RESTAURANT NAME)

LOCATION:

WITH WHO:

WHAT I ORDERED:

MY REVIEW (COLOR THE STARS)
☆ ☆ ☆ ☆ ☆

LOCATION:

WITH WHO:

WHAT I ORDERED:

MY REVIEW
☆ ☆ ☆ ☆ ☆

LOCATION:

WITH WHO:

WHAT I ORDERED:

MY REVIEW
☆ ☆ ☆ ☆ ☆

LOCATION:

WITH WHO:

WHAT I ORDERED:

MY REVIEW
☆ ☆ ☆ ☆ ☆

LOCATION:

WITH WHO:

WHAT I ORDERED:

MY REVIEW
☆ ☆ ☆ ☆ ☆

LOCATION:

WITH WHO:

WHAT I ORDERED:

MY REVIEW
☆ ☆ ☆ ☆ ☆

Made in the USA
Las Vegas, NV
30 January 2024